THE MASTERY OF LIFE
A Course in Selflove

Waltraud Kuon

About the author

Waltraud Kuon, born 1957 in Bad Saulgau, in Baden-Württemberg, Germany.

For the past 30 years, Waltraud Kuon has been working in her own practice for psychosomatic physical therapy.

She lived in Berlin from 1978-1997 until the Allgäuer mountains summoned her.

In 2005, her dream came true to live her life close to the water.
Already as a child, the ferry boats on Lake Constance touched a soft spot in her heart.
Eventually, she followed her inner voice.

Today she lives in Meersburg and works in Salem.

THE MASTERY OF LIFE
A Course in Selflove

The Key to the Gateway of Life
is the Light of Love

Waltraud Kuon

© 2016 Waltraud Kuon

Translation:
Jean Klaus

Proof reader:
Wilma Sommer
Paul Chodak

Layout:
Angela Petani

Book-Cover Design:
Christiane Marber

Illustrations:
Franziska Lorenz

On Cover Images:
123RF GmbH

Flowerpicture (page 43):
nongkran_ch – Fotolia.com

Production and publishing:
BoD – Books on Demand, Norderstedt
ISBN: 9-783749-436620

Acknowledgements

Heartfelt thanks to all those who encouraged me to put my dreams, inspirations and good thoughts down on paper.

This book has been written thanks to the dear friends Nele, Angela, Christiane, Ingrid, Franziska, Jean and Wilma and my friends Frank, Markus and Paul.

The path was a wonderful one, filled with joy, enthusiasm and many improvements from heaven above.

Index

The Mastery of Life
A Course in Selflove

The Key to the Gate of Life
is the Light of Love

Lay your hands on your heart everyday and get in touch with yourself. Speak words of acknowledgement and direct them into your inner self. Say something nice to yourself. You will become brighter within yourself and feel lighter! Build up a loving relationship with yourself which shines internally and externally and gives free reign to a heart that is full of life and to your own life.

Take the first step today:

"I ask to be able in my imperfection to love, respect and accept myself. And I ask to be able to love and respect myself with all my inadequacies as well as my strengths and weaknesses."

Say and direct it within yourself:

10 times – 100 times – 1000 times

Allow your soul to become a personality.

Become aware of your negative characteristics leading you astray. Free yourself from them.

Form your soul anew.

To give the human being the courage to get going and find his talents along his individual way is a matter close to my heart. It is my wish for him that he lets go of the destructive fears, frees himself from painful habits and is able to lead a happy and independent life.

Each and every person is capable of doing good things and good deeds. Perhaps he's lost faith in himself, thinks very little of himself, and has forgotten who he truly is. He doesn't need to become anybody else. A person can't change his original self and will never be able to. With courage however, he can bring down the walls and open himself up to life anew. In his centre he is exactly as life needs him.

Life needs YOU especially!

The words of R.W. Emerson touch me deeply:

"Everyone holds society for being more clever than his soul and doesn't know that the soul – his soul – is wiser than the whole world."

I would like to guide people in how to love themselves. It is this love of self that fulfills the soul and offers protection along their journey which they take with responsibility and self-determination.

The soul can grow and develop only under the protective blanket of love and help others to be strong and to cope with life.

I no longer want to neglect saying what's most important in a person's life. It is learning to love, respect and acknowledge one´s self. Valuable human beings take valuable steps.

Never give up hope!

Valuable steps that serve all of creation, need permanent impulses from open hearts and inspiration – inspiration from the cosmos through the spirit of creation, which inflames the soul.

Along his way a person learns

to f e e l and to l i s t e n ...

Who is that behind the wall?

"It seemed as if a strange spirit was raging in me destroying my soul."

Completely helpless and full of fear I shut all the doors going out to life.

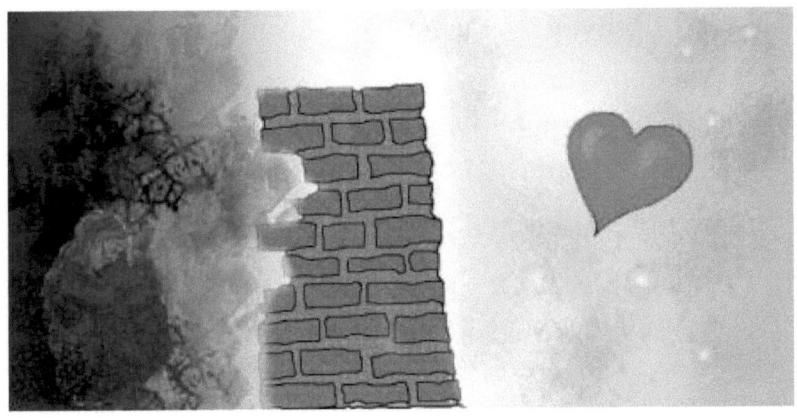

"This Life" as it was, meant only fear.

It all started in early childhood when during the night, dark shadows tore at my throat wanting to pull out my soul. I was afraid that one day they would gain victory over me.

I didn't know then that the loss of the soul meant the end of liveliness.

I wasn't experiencing any protection, so I thought, and my fighting spirit was weary.

In my darkest and most threatening hour, exhausted, I saw myself at the mercy of the gloomy forces, I felt a bright light above me and to my right. An angel called my name with a loud voice and spoke:

"Pray the Lord's Prayer! The devil can't tolerate that!"

And I prayed: "Our Father who art in Heaven …"

At the word – Heaven –, I didn't get any further, the shadow lost its power, was pulled away from me, sucked into a vortex, that overpowered it.

The light dissolved the darkness into pure nothing.

From that hour on I knew that if angels intercede on my behalf to keep the devil off my back, my life must have a purpose.

The powers of heaven and earth have been leading me through a hell on earth.

I often lay for hours on the floor praying, crying, screaming, begging God to help me.

Difficult days outweighed the good days.

I no longer understood the world.

I can't go on this way.

If not so – how then?

How does life work?

My prayers were answered. On one of the good days I came across a book containing lessons which were not easy for me to accept. My old destructive mind was to be replaced by a new and constructive one. For hours, months I practised putting this message into action:

"Love, respect and acknowledge yourself from deep inside your heart," it read.

I stood in front of the mirror in my bathroom, lit a candle, looked into my eyes and told myself that I would love, respect and acknowledge myself.

I felt pain in my chest as I saw these strange and staring eyes.

It appeared that my heart had to turn over in order to be able to hear this message.

And it turned over several times. It released itself from its old rigid anchoring and put itself into a totally new position, with its face turned outward. From now on it wanted to be able to touch the light of life.

For hours I held out standing in front of the mirror. Until then I had never looked into my eyes with this intensity. It was only with the help of learned breathing techniques that I could endure the pain. Tears running down my face and with weak knees I remained in this position which seemed like an eternity. I recognized the mental harshness towards myself and my soul and saw that a pure and beautiful face hid behind a mask terribly distorted with fear.

Ice-cold thoughts and words of rejection and condemnation had closed up my heart and for many years frightened my soul so that it drifted off into other worlds without bodily contact. Back then I believed I was losing my mind. This was a bitter experience, and sometimes out of fear my heart was close to stopping. I was deathly afraid for myself and for my future. I was really scared of everybody and everything. I barricaded myself behind walls.

My decision to take a totally new course was certain

Along with making my new decisions, life provided me with the right and important human beings at my side. By "coincidence" and angel-like, they crossed my paths and with gentle hints let me know which steps to take next.

I did my homework diligently and didn't miss a day without placing my hands on my heart, saying something nice to myself, in the beginning just wanting to be by myself for a few minutes, having some peace and quiet.

10 times, 100 times, 1000 times I spoke good and warming words of love, respect and acknowledgement into myself. Strange and wondrous worlds of emotions were opened up to me. I felt life, good life.

I became aware that words and thoughts could change my life.

Until this realization, I believed the whole world was one bad and enormous threat.

Everything was totally different.

What was going on in *my* inner world determined the experiences in the outer world. This meant that *I* could create an entirely different life to the one dictated to me until then.

My heart became lighter. Something expanded within me and enthusiasm moved in.

The ice inside me broke up piece by piece. It melted away like butter in the warm sunshine.

I told myself that *I* was good, worked diligently, and that *I* was making an effort to reach a divine consciousness. Yes, *I* wanted God, the redeemer, love, the WAY, to find exactly that which would free me from the rigid world of ideas of my childhood and youth. A fundamental law of life had revealed itself to me: "In the beginning was the Word, and the Word was with God, and the Word was God. And everything that was created was created by the Word." (Joh. 1:1) It is the thought and spoken word that matters. I felt strengthened, when I put words of love into myself.

That year I turned 39.

I will always remember this year in my life. The realization that I could redesign my life and my world through a single thought, fascinated me. I was able to be instrumental in life. I could trace back my negative experiences to my inferior thoughts. When it came to thinking I was always a champion. Now it depended upon the direction my thinking would take. This was as plain as daylight: "I would give my life an altogether new direction!" My life as a victim would soon come to an end.

People need role models

My father was a man of large stature and noble character, who cried when sad and asked forgiveness when he made a mistake. He was genuine, humble and affectionate. He followed his heart and showed absolute greatness in his thoughts and actions. Already as a young person, I admired him for his strength and his courage not to be ashamed of showing his feelings.

How could it happen that we lost touch with each other? On my way – back to my heart – we found each other again.

I undertook to no longer deny my feelings. I cried when I was sad. Regardless of all the self-controlled people around me, I expressed the feelings I had feared for so many years. What I held inside should be able to be expressed whenever the necessity and need arises.

If I felt embarrassment in showing my feelings, I practised dealing with embarrassment. If my feelings caused me to feel ashamed, I wanted to learn to endure and understand shame.

One thing was for sure: Until the day I die, I vowed to myself, I would live in truth, become free in my thinking and emotional world and see to it that my heart remained open.

From now on I lived *my* life.

I allowed myself every single emotion. And I was willing, no matter what it costs, to open myself up for myself. There was a complete change in my facial expression, it became more alert and clear. The beauty within appeared layer by layer. And life felt full of vitality. When I looked in the mirror I somehow saw "the real me".

This "real me" hadn't yet found a stable and well anchored position then. It was in need of growth. I was constantly on the lookout, listening, watching and feeling in order to train my authenticity to be centred and remain centred and to be responsible for being my inner best friend.

I searched for myself and found myself

For years I looked for myself in the distance and now found myself deep down inside.

A path full of events opened up for me. At times it led me over a course of detours, extensive and full of suspense, but finally breathtakingly successful and into *my own* independent life, free from the opinions of others. The door to freedom and truth was opened more and more.

I was very anxious and curious as to how people would react to my new behaviour, being aware of my feelings, thinking for myself and not saying yes to everyone. I was afraid of rejection. It turned out to be the opposite. I received respect and attention. I was no longer "just nice and good". Occasionally, I was even unpleasant. But I showed my unaltered, true character. People quickly recognized that I always let them know what I felt deep down inside of me. From then on, I was consulted as an honest mentor.

My satisfaction affected every area of my life. When one's own inner treasure is brought up from the depths in the form of pure truth and can be seen, one experiences respect and appreciation for oneself and for all others.

The Angels assist us

and we can hear them, if we are willing to leave the old, incurable and destructive ways behind. When we become pure and gentle, we can tune into them. We can find them in a world of tender silence. Those who find the courage to show their sensitivity and vulnerability are in resonance with the angels and are likewise borne by them.

Along my journey finding myself, I noticed how many human beings didn't have the courage to show their real selves.

I wouldn't have been ready voluntarily to leave the ways of feigned strength, rawness and excessive demands. This corresponded to my character up until then. The distress I was feeling, my fear of failure and my desperation forced me to make a new decision. By looking at things through the eyes of my heart, with understanding, I had to admit that I couldn't have everything without eventually breaking down. And so I chose a frugal, simple and peaceful life instead of inconsiderate needs of the ego that wanted everything. There's a saying, "he who wants everything, loses everything". Much later the angels let it be known that happiness is to be found in frugality and simplicity.

The idea to hoard material things and possessions didn't bring me any happiness.

"A bag full of money doesn't by any means guarantee a warm and happy nest", as my wise and clever father used to say.

I searched for myself and found myself in the gentle and tenderness of feelings. One day everyone will find themself. We are searching for the fulfilling wealth which is within us. We are not looking for material goods alone; this path is not a true one. If it is chosen after a disappointment, it is misleading. It is not possible to find love and recognition through material things. However, each person decides for himself which way of life he chooses.

God, who is love, gives us a free will. God/Love knows no punishment. God/Love loves.

Though it can hurt when we lose our way along the path of a life of love, we can turn around and with understanding begin anew.

This process of change and looking into one's self can extend over several years or even decades.

For sure, I could never have gone along this path on my own. I prayed for hours and talked with my earthly and my supernatural guardians, my angels here on earth, the human beings, and the divine light-beings beyond the earth. I asked them to stand by me on my path and to withstand the challenges. My earth-angels, by that I mean my dearest friends, believed in me, and my celestial helpers whispered in my left ear, the ear of my heart, and strengthened my backbone with boundless courage.

You too can also be sure that they will whisper in your ear and likewise strengthen your backbone with courage.

Know who you are

My valuable earth-angels, gentle, angel-like
creatures of flesh and blood, gave me highest
esteem.

My wonderful girlfriends and my beloved friend
called me

a beloved child of God.

What could be worthier

than to be a beloved child of God.

All of us are his beloved children.

"You are his daughter."

"You are his son."

At this stage of my life, I became aware of how
important it was to have friends with a healthy
mentality close at hand, to take us by the hand and
lead us over life's troubled waters.

Little by little, I felt confirmed and accepted in my
SINCERITY and *HONESTY* by some higher and
greater love. And in my heart, I knew that deep
inside all human beings are upright and good and
chosen by God who is love.

The final attacks

The final attacks against myself, the rejection, self-destruction and self-doubt that still remained were appeased by the love in my heart and changed into acceptance, self-esteem and a deep belief in the good in myself and in all other human beings.

I spoke to myself with enthusiasm 10 times – 100 times – 1000 times the warm words of love, respect and acknowledgement well aware of the rich returns.

And every single time an indescribable energy passed through me. It forced walls to break down.

How many protective barriers can a child build up to his adult life?

And how many years does an adult need to break down all these walls?

The healthier and more focused I became, the louder and clearer I could hear the angels' voices. And I perceived their messages as

Signposts for every person on our planet:

"We are watching out for you with a love beyond measure. If you've made a decision for the good, you may be very sure of it."

"We aren't able to help every human being. Those who choose evil and darkness over love and light, and likewise those who don't believe in angels, are moving far away from the frequency of light and love."

Today, I am aware that the angels never abandon their beloved humans. It is the humans who distance themselves from the angels.

Already as a child, the guardian angels spoke to me and touched my back, pushed me forward and up the stairs.

At that time, I thought it was the same for everyone. There was no reason whatsoever to talk about it. I took it for granted that the angels watched over us and had fun playing with us.

I would like to give you a picture of how the angels appear in my life today

I notice them in lots of human beings as their "golden souls". I "see" them in human beings as pure yellow, gold and also as a white light in various shapes and sizes, as their true inner nature. Likewise, I "feel" the light of the angels as a guardian-angel beside the human beings. Up until now I haven't noticed "wings". When I find myself in a phase of intense connectivity with heaven and its winds, I sense their highly sensitive vibrations. I'm able to do this through an intensive breathing technique with a volume of seven litres.

God has given me this wonderful gift. And he has asked me to establish a way of life and existence for these almost dead and lost souls. "Help these people on earth to come alive and find their way. Fill their hearts with love and say something kind to them", he added.

At this point, I have allowed myself to write about my calling.

You too can find the courage to search for your calling

We are born into a family in which each member differs from the other like the fingers on a hand. Trying to be just like someone else means failure and leads to an unhappy life.

Be yourself, authentic, honest, direct and clear! Speak your truth! Find the right tone! Genuine and upright human beings with a healthy mind have become rare.

Look inside yourself and listen! Search for your calling! Go deep down within to find yourself! The treasure always lies at the bottom. If you haven't found your treasure yet, could it be that you've just been scratching the surface? Breathe, breathe, breathe! Lay your hands upon your heart and put loving thoughts into it. Love is the light for your spirit, that allows you to see. Get to the bottom and find out what's there!

Note: When you find yourself not making progress, not getting anywhere, then it's time to dig deeper.

Life needs every loving heart in order to create a harmonious world. Life needs YOU.

Don't wait too long. Get going and notice how it feels to run head-on into the wall!

Fall down and get up again! Fall 100 times, but get up 101 times! Ask big personalities, public figures, how often they have got up again! Your vitality dies when you try to be perfect. Perfection means fitting yourself into a mould and nailing down the victory you've achieved.

Try it out, start over again and have another go at it! Stay focused on respect and love. If you're not successful, continue feeling within. You have made gains through this valuable experience. Be daring to leave the old, ineffective, useless ways.

Don't live beyond your means! That has got many human beings into trouble. Live a simple life! Stretch your limitations in order to get in touch with yourself, to perceive yourself! Don't wait until you can do something perfectly. If there were only human beings without flaws out there, the streets would be empty. The woods would be silent if no birds sang except those that sing best.

Be able to feel that sometimes you don't feel anything! Everything is good just the way it is!

Go forward step by step! Take notice of life or don't!

Open your heart over and over again. Become sensitive, tactful and gentle in feeling. By doing so you proceed to the frequency of the breath of love.

This is where the body, mind and soul joyously resonate in harmony with one another. You have reached the destination of your journey and have arrived at the foundation of heartfelt love.

You are qualified and now ready to put your talent to work. It is granted to you in trust that you will live up to it and will fulfill it with love.

How much a person achieves is not what matters. The big question life asks of us is: are we doing the work with all our heart? Every single activity should be made wholeheartedly.

Life asks of you that you take each and every step together with your heart. Don't undertake anything halfheartedly or without heart. If you choose paths, that are grudgingly demanding of you, you will become ill. Don't be everybody's darling. Heartless actions and heartless steps don't have any meaning. Pointless undertakings that aren't of service to the earth and the living beings on it are useless or cause harm. Never sell your heart! Whoever sells his heart will soon sell his earth for money that he hasn't earned honestly with his talent. Always keep in mind that sooner or later we will reap what we have sown.

We are what we eat

During the course of our lifetime our bodies, upon which we play our life melody, should become like a finely tuned Stradivarius, (named after A. Stradivari, 1644 - 1737). It is recommended that you take great care of your instrument. The soul, which resonates like the sounds of a Stradivarius, wishes to live in harmony with the body.

The body is the most important "dwelling place" in which we soul-spirit beings spend our earthly existence. By keeping it clean and appreciating it, it will gladly serve us for a long time.

An essential aspect along a person's rescue path is his nutrition. Discipline and abstinence, fasting and occasional going without something form a person's character. A person who takes himself seriously, who loves himself, regards himself with respect. He doesn't ruin his health with junk food. Fatty and sugary foods and over acidified drinks clog up the pores and deprive him of his ability for enthusiasm.

If you want to discover your nature then comply with it:

Eat things that are green, yellow, red and multicoloured. Be at one with nature. Eat what grows in the ground and on top of it.

Remain permeable!

The angels are calling: "Don't waste any time."

The deepest concern they have for us human beings here on earth is, that we should learn to love, respect and acknowledge ourselves.

"Get started today," is what they wish.

The light that becomes bigger and brighter in Selflove, self-respect and acknowledgement, is the key for the gate to our own heart. Through the hearts' open doors flows a pure current from the universe immediately into our core and joins us with the great cosmic current bringing about "enthusiasm" everywhere.

By comparing this strong current of the cosmic spirit to the electricity that causes the wires of all the lightbulbs to light up, it is able to light up every heart.

If you want to have personal magnetism, then stay in connection with the cosmic current!

This is the spirit-soul

"All you need to do is open up your heart, let the love be seen and the spirit will come to you." It will fuel your thoughts (breathe! breathe! breathe!) and this spurring-on will brighten the soul so that your life can become enthusiastic for you and the world. All great things have come into being through enthusiasm.

Daily we find ourselves in the school of life

It wants to guide us well through life with the help of some life-rules:

Love, respect and acknowledge yourself and your fellow human beings with all your heart! Love is the essence of life. Without love there is nothing but emptiness.

Be thankful! Gratitude sets the life of a person on healthy and stable legs. Gratitude opens the gates to the kingdom of heaven. By giving thanks you increase your credit, by complaining you increase your debit. That which is within appears outward.

Learn to ask! It is within man's nature to want to help. A person who is allowed to help finds fulfillment. By asking we make another person happy; for he is needed and may give.

Live honestly!
"The truth will set you free."
(Joh. 8, 32)
There is only one truth, the truth of the heart. It sets the conscience free. A good conscience is a soft pillow to rest upon.

Forgiveness heals all wounds. Forgive yourself and your neighbour! In order to be able to practice forgiveness, we have to be offended ourselves and likewise offend another. If a person hasn't been hurt, then he can't practice forgiveness.

Everybody, according to his level of knowledge and development, makes mistakes. We are all in the school of life, and are learning till the last day of our life. The challenge is to persevere in recognizing destructive traits and continue learning through experience to become a wiser person.

Without a doubt, I unknowingly caused human beings harm during my lifetime. I didn't know any better. And that's how it is for everyone.

It was crucial for me to forgive myself for these small and larger offences and to exercise understanding for myself. Because I was able to forgive myself, I offered myself a handshake. It's hard to believe how eagerly our soul awaits a

"please forgive me for not having listened to you."
Amid tears, the harshness deep within me dissolved.

It goes without saying that today I reflect and look back at my mistakes, forgive myself and my fellow human beings. When the harm inflicted upon me becomes too imposing in my life, then I find forgiveness impossible. I then ask for help through the strength of God:

"Dear God, please help me, you do it. I can't and don't want to forgive. I'm not strong enough. The harm that has been unjustly inflicted upon me has thrown me off track. Please dear God, forgive them for they don't know what they've done to me!" I let go and hand it over. If God accepts my suffering heart then everything will work out for the best. And my backpack that was carrying the *heavy* offence, is emptied. My "back" becomes *light and free.*

I continued on my way

Curious and overjoyed due to my achieved victories, I now found myself before the next higher step in the lesson of Selflove

Love says: "Everything has a purpose."

Life has taught me and still teaches me today, to accept everything without resistance and to love what is at the moment.

Instead of avoiding the challenge, I take it by the hand in order to take a closer look at the seemingly "bad thing". Most of the time the fear underneath it disappears as I look more closely. As long as I don't deal with the challenge head-on, it keeps following me, wearing me out, until I give up and accept it. It's all good in the end. If it's not yet good, then I haven't reached the end. Life allows me enough time, however, I don't want to waste another meaningless hour of my life.

Every challenge is good for something. Without challenge there would never be a learning process or progress.

Life is always right. In resisting, we lose our strength and in the end have to admit: "I've had enough. Then it should just happen the way it's meant to."

What will be, will be. If we fight against the wisdom and intelligence of life, we will fail. We have to go along with life. In letting go, things turn out well as life intended. Life is the love that wants the very best for us.

Later on, when looking back, we can thank life that everything worked out in the best way for us.

After all, we see only a part, whereas life sees the full picture.

This realization has become one of the strongest in my life so far.

In resistance there is neither victory nor peace.

"It is what it is," says love; it doesn't judge.

I let go and let God carry out his plan for my life. In doing so I remain the doer. God is working through me and gives me the strength to fulfill his plans for my life.

"And my angels are leading the way shaping a successful and prosperous path for me."

Yes, this is how I'll do it! This is how life works!

These thoughts feel good!

Everyday determine the path of life anew!

I was constantly rushing around from one place to another. Restless and untiring I was unconsciously chasing after an indefinable ideal.

One day I saw myself from the outside looking in rushing and running around.

I stopped and stood in the middle of the path and asked life where I'm rushing off to. Life didn't answer me.

Soon the answer came to me in a dream.

An angel spoke to me: "Slow down! You don't need to pressure yourself. Just follow your path! The true and inner life does not look for your success or for your facade. All it wants is you, your spirit, your soul and your heart! "

"Go quietly and slowly, contemplatively and with care. Step by step. You will be guided."

"Listen to the voice inside you. Life is speaking to you through your heart."

I learned how to speak with my heart

Over time, I was able to trust my heart's voice more and more. At first, it was unfamiliar. But the more loving words I placed in my heart, the clearer I heard the answer. I spoke to my heart in a fine and gentle language: "My wonderful heart, is everything ok? You are my life and within you I find the power of love. For your service to me I give you thanks. Because of you thousands of litres of blood are pumping through me day after day, and you never complain. You are magnificent. I love you!"

It raises our spirits when we feed ourselves loving thoughts and words. They satisfy and fulfill us:

"I love, respect and acknowledge myself with my whole heart."

10 times, 100 times, 1000 times I spoke these words to myself.

Now and then my craving for love lost its power. My physical energy grew immeasurable. The good words of love, respect and acknowledgement bestowed upon me an enormous amount of strength and nourished my hungry soul.

Where is heaven?

In a dream, I saw an image that depicted a grey shadow within a soul, coming from my centre and inside of me a voice called: "You out there, come inside and fill the remaining darkness in you with the spirit of love and with a light that shines like gold. Help other dark souls, who encounter you in their fear to fill themselves with light that shines

like gold and with words of love.
This is your purpose in life!"

Heaven is within ourselves, was proclaimed to me. ("The kingdom of God is within you, today, here and now." Luk. 17,20-21)

In the spirit of Selflove, I should work towards this heaven from the outside and from above like a laser beam to the divine foundation, I was told. To this day, I have been following these instructions lovingly.

The life of a person changes radically when he realizes that he becomes that which he thinks of himself and of others.

10 times, 100 times, 1000 times I spoke words of love and good to myself and others to fill up the "holes" and brighten up the grey shadows. And indeed, heaven opened up.

It is an immense gift that everything we need to know is revealed to us, but on one condition: that we increasingly do without headphones and constant noise streaming.

If we can perk up our ears like curious children do and listen very carefully to the silence, life delivers an answer to every one of our questions. We are never left alone for a second, whether day or night.

What is there to be afraid of?

I came to realize that my fears would surface when I wasn't living accordingly and not following the voice of my heart.

I wanted to become more awake and attentive.

When the heart is lacking in love, fear takes over, impairing the soul. The soul is dependent on the flow of love from an open heart.

This love is a protective shell for the soul.

Butterflies in the heart – butterflies in the stomach

My life became free and easy. I was floating on happiness. Although I was flying with the butterflies, I still felt lonely.

If you dare to fly too high, you run into the danger of crashing.

And I crashed again and again, down onto the ground and had to pick myself up again. But then one night I had a dream about "contact through grounding" (see detailed explanation p. 52-53).

Well-grounded, in connection with the world and its creatures, I felt stable. For the first time in my life, I was well aware of the impressive influence which healthy grounding had on my life. I stopped falling down.

Heavenly Father, where would I be without you and your angels?

"I love my life and my life loves me!"

My growing belief in myself and the good in man made me more secure. In complete new trust, I was able to approach people, free of inhibition. And I trusted myself to look people in the eye, which up until then had been completely inconceivable.

My positive experiences encouraged me and lured me out into "the world". In my wildest dreams I couldn't have imagined that I'd one day find freedom of fear at the bottom of my heart and want to embrace myself and the whole world.

Endure a standstill

I wanted to continue bravely in a forward direction.
And then suddenly the past caught up with me. I
literally went around the challenges in circles,
around and around and around. I didn't move one
centimetre forwards.

After a long period of feeling irritated and in a bad
mood, I paused for a moment asking my inner self
what this stagnation meant.

"You're running ahead of your life at breakneck
speed. Set the pace which coincides with the pace of
life! Take small steps! Already things aren't going
fast enough for you and again you think that you
aren't enough. Life doesn't agree with that: look
back and recognize the many small and yet
considerable achievements, and thank yourself for
your abundant power of endurance and your
unlimited courage! Don't take the next step forward
until you've done this! Be aware of your
accomplishments! Not until you realize your efforts
up until now, can they carry you into the future with
your head held high. Where are you running to and
why? If you can't acknowledge yourself along the
way, then you'll never be able to. Therefore, take
time to pause, endure the standstill and love, respect
and acknowledge yourself with all your heart."

The energy that I drew from recognizing my little achievements carried me on and once again forwards. What a refreshing realization!

Use the strength of the healing spirit in your head

"I saw the light."

A complete inner change took place within me, away from being destructive and towards being considerate with gentle reflection.

This new world, a head filled with healing spirit working together with a heart full of light, feels good. And so, as a result, I'm good for all other creatures. Everything that happens in my adult life has its beginning *within me*. *I* take full responsibility for every single thought that determines my world. *I'm the one* who thinks, and *I'm the one* who experiences what's been thought. *I am the building designer of my life.*

I will no longer allow those wild, uncontrollable, demonic thoughts to rage in me. My consciousness has reached a higher level of development. I am the master of my thoughts. And may heaven quicken me by day and by night with its inspiration. I will be present and listen very carefully in the stillness.

I feel my inner cleanliness

Harmony

When my spirit-soul and my body found themselves in harmony, I no longer liked wearing any black clothing. Emotionally, that would throw me back into my hiding place. The light that I needed on my skin and inside me couldn't reach me when wearing black clothing.

The light which shines through light-coloured or colourful clothes lifts my spirit on gloomy days.

My former dependence caused me to suffer

My silent cry for love showed itself outwardly in the form of a crooked spine.

Today happiness and love are very active within me. I have learned to fulfill my life on my own, to stand up for myself and to be positive, open and honest with myself.

I give away love and happiness from my newly gained inner wealth.

I encounter people through love and they answer with love.

Because I accept myself, I feel accepted.

Because I feel accepted, I am able to accept everyone else.

Because I love myself, I feel loved.

Because I feel loved, I am able to love each and every person.

Treating myself with kindness and respect makes it possible for me to treat all other people likewise with kindness and respect.

The world has become full of colour –
and I'm blooming within it

I am happy.

I am thankful.

I am free.

I listen to my heart and follow its instructions.

I believe unwaveringly in the truth of my heart.

It speaks a clear, pure and simple language.

In peaceful silence, I'll listen and pour love, respect and acknowledgement into it, and I'm sure it likes to "communicate" with me.

I mustn't ever let my heart become empty again

With a fulfilled heart, I am happy and satisfied with myself and with the world.

Every day I place my hands on my heart and speak words of love, respect and acceptance to myself.

"I love, respect and acknowledge myself with my whole heart!"

10 times – 100 times – 1000 times

A bright light flows through me altering the cells in my body, filling every single cell with light and love, cleansing my thoughts and words.

The love in my heart spills over and fills up my soul from head to toe. With feet firmly planted on the ground, the soul will find its anchorage and so land on earth.

My life has become so beautiful.

Our loving spirit is constantly creating within us a deeper, additional and bigger space in which a new life filled with strength can take place. The depth of this space seems unfathomable. This is where the connection with the origin of all life, all works and all miracles takes place.

The immeasurable and creative energy we've received from this loving source affects all of us.

From the deepest primary fundament, heaven, God grants man the mercy of love.

Should we decide to become warm hearted, meek, benevolent, kind and calm, our body, spirit and soul will be able to heal.

In this peaceful state, we are able to hear heaven's will.

It's a good idea if we make its will our will:

"Love your neighbour as yourself." (Mk. 12, 99)

Under the protective sheath of love, a soul can grow into a personality.

A person's worth develops and grows with love. A person who knows his worth doesn't sacrifice himself for a little bit of recognition. He is faithful in his self-respect, and he doesn't fall into disrepair by trying to do more than he can cope with. He doesn't throw his life away. He's aware that life wishes to be lived and loved, shaped by himself.

Looking back, I see that I've been successful in opening the gate to the light of life by knocking down a massive stonework. It was the barrier between my mind and my heart. A misguided mind thought words of destruction and my heart had to put up a barrier to protect me from these harsh words. Back then my negative-thinking head refused to listen to my heart. This was a typical manifestation of the ego that said: "I can do everything better than love can."

Ego is love's enemy. It wants to make us worthless. It causes separation and loneliness. It leads us into despair and finds joy when we founder.

Don't give ego a chance!

When it catches up with you, defeat it by asking if you're looking for a power play or helping love to win.

When I was in doubt, I sat down and went within myself to get in touch with love. I asked my heart: "How would you decide in this situation?" The answers were astounding and were altogether different from what I had expected. That was the end of my ego. And hereby my ego lost all power over me.

Trust the light and love in your heart!

The creative strength of spirit is a blessing, a godsend. *Your* heart's good intention, *your* untiring work and *your firm belief in yourself* can open doors, cause walls to crumble, and when necessary, move mountains.

Breathing – I also call it – inner development

"For every disease there is a previous thought!"

The development and disentanglement of the sick cells, having lost all harmony with other cells, happens in such a way:

During deep relaxation you try to find out what the sick thought is, and locate the area in your body where this sick thought is attacking the cells (please breath into the sick area). By breathing into this area, it is brought from the dark subconsciousness into the light of consciousness. In a quiet place, a person will hear what comes. The ill mind is able to be changed at any moment. Deformed cells can be consciously influenced through healing words. These healing words then lead to harmonious feelings and these feelings heal the cells.

"Each and every cell of my body is filled with pure divine light and with pure divine love." In moments of disharmony I speak these words many times to myself and notice how within a short period of time my nerves become calm.

The holy = healing spirit is above all.

It causes all cells to revive.

A human being who has humiliated himself and therefore made himself sick is blessed in that he is able, through love, to get back up again.

Breath = soul = white smoke must fill the body from head to toe.

By having learnt to no longer be a target for the assaults coming from the darkness of the world, I know the importance of protecting my soul by being securely anchored.

If you train deep breathing daily, ground yourself intensely, your soul cannot be wrested from the body.

The dark shadows mainly become active in breathless moments of excessive demands and self-doubt.

When you love, respect and acknowledge yourself, the soul is happy and well-anchored in your body right down to the soles of your feet.

Every darkness, fold, crevice and groove should be opened and freed from old waste by means of breathing.

If the soul is brought up to full size, all existential fears disappear.

Overweightness is often the sign of an ungrounded soul which tries to ground itself through excessive weight.

We have to see to it that we never run out of air.

The one who has the longer breath will persevere.

The wind shapes and changes the world.

All creatures are served by the same
Wind = Breath = Soul.

In this way, they overcome the challenges.

Take a deep breath and meet the challenge.

Grounding

The world needs people who have **both feet firmly planted on the ground**.

And the world needs people who **stand up for what they believe in**.

When we are continuously and consciously connected to Mother Earth, we are guaranteed secure ground under our feet.

My experience teaches me to make sure that I ground myself daily.

By concentrating, please place both feet on the ground, outside or in the living room or office and feel the surface under your feet.

Imagine that you were a strong and healthy tree with a very deep-reaching root system. Your roots are stretching deeper and deeper into the earth giving you solid support. Breathe intensively through your whole body from head to foot and down into your roots. In this way you connect well with Mother Earth.

Well grounded people stay calm during life's worst storms. They are standing on good ground.

People who are grounded are nice to be around, whereas the ones who have lost their footing, so to say, tend to be difficult, annoying, irritating and are not fun to be with and therefore we feel uncomfortable in their presence. They may even cause others to become sick. Lying often plays a part in their lives.

When the human soul tells a lie or is lied to, its soul shrinks, becomes smaller and therefore is no longer within the legs and feet touching the ground. The soul-legs are too short in order to ground. Liars don't get far in life because sooner or later their lies catch up with them.

Human beings who aren't grounded are, so to say, "hanging in the air". They are afflicted with problems and fears and all too easily pull others onto their track to a dangerous life without roots.

Human beings who have lost their grounding no longer feel the love in their hearts. And without this grounding, the magnetic field of the heart is unbearable.

As a result, these people feel insecure, confused and helpless. In their fear, they lose direction and touch with reality. We'd like to say to them: "Get your feet back on the ground!"

When well connected to the earth, our body functions like a lightning rod. The tension we are charged with (anger, pressure etc.) wants to be conducted to earth by the shortest route possible.

Take long walks in the forest.

I felt like I was dead inside –
now I'm alive again!

The most important work in a person's life is the work he does on himself, the development of his capability to love.

The way in which we treat ourselves is the basis for how we treat all other creatures.

Fear drives us to behave towards others in a harmful way, but harming ourselves first. Through the experiences so far in my life, I've learnt that the fear, which almost devoured my soul, was responsible for my struggles and weaknesses (sickness).

The heart's love dissolved all the fears.

All hearts of all creatures on God's beautiful earth should be able to live free of fear, peacefully and happily.

Before I broke down the remaining thin wall from the inside, I assured myself that love's light would protect me from any new wounds.

I never want to have to "wall" myself in again.

It turned out differently:

On the way out into the open, I came to the realization, that suffering and pain are part of a life lived in honesty.

However, my perspective had changed in the meantime:

With new awareness, I see today that what had been harming me in the past was the inner war of others, those with sick minds. These sick individuals haven't found themselves yet and aren't at peace with themselves. When they hurt somebody, it comes from their sick minds. They are not conscious, that their own thoughts never leave their own nervous system. Their sick behaviour only harms themselves. They aren't aware of what they're doing. Unconsciously, they treat others in the same way they treat themselves. They are their own worst enemy. And they see all others as enemies. They don't live in their own hearts. They don't live in love. They are always at war with themselves and others. They too should learn to take responsibility for their thoughts, words and deeds. Everything we send out comes back to us like a boomerang. We reap what we sow.

So now, when I feel slighted and it hits my heart like a poisoned arrow, I react instantly. I've learned to be aware of my feelings and to stand up for myself. I am worth it. I make it very clear to the person that he's gone too far and polluted my inner space. In very plain language, I define for him my healthy boundaries and ask for an apology. If this isn't possible or doesn't happen, then I let go, place the hurt in God's hands and adjourn to my inner path of peace. My mind, my soul and my heart can stay healthy only when I am at peace. Today I am able to protect myself in every dangerous situation, as a lioness protects her cub.

For years I've been touched by the tale of

"The Little Prince"
(Antoine de Saint-Exupéry "The Little Prince"):

"One sees clearly only with the heart!"

How very true!

I am grateful for the truth, love's light, that it has worked in me and will continue working. I look at life today through entirely different eyes, eyes of love and my sunny heart.

"I was blind and now I can see!" (Joh. 9, 25)

At this point, some doubters might want to say that I've lost touch with reality. I would like to say to all those doubters, that the world is good. All creatures could live safe and secure and within the happy and gentle breath of love. So many people in the world have lost themselves and their grounding, just as I had lost touch with myself, reality and the truth. I needed help, to be understood. I didn't need to be judged.

Life keeps on calling me back:

"Change your focus! Encourage people, build them up! Direct the energy, so that it knows where it should take you and others!

Stay on course headed towards love!

Become love itself!"

How favourably and friendly our heart's truth shapes our life

A heart filled with love enjoys the success of a friend. It is happy when the neighbour has a lucky experience. It grieves with those who are sad. It weeps with the despondent and has the strength to lay the souls at the end of their time here on earth in God's glory. And it has been granted the gift to take away the fear of death from the living and the dying.

Love has many faces. Sometimes love reacts like a small child. It kisses flowers and loves how snow sparkles in the sunlight. It is content, free and always makes it a point to use the mind to bring about good.

Today I kneel down before "God our Father", the boundless light of creation, that sustains all life in love. I kneel down before the almighty cosmic "Holy Spirit", which fuels and inspires our thoughts, and through us has a healing effect on creation. I kneel down before "God's son", his child Jesus, who has given us the awareness of the infinite healing power of love and unconditional forgiveness, from person to person.

We need God's help and God needs us

With deep humility, I acknowledge that we need heavenly guidance as well as the protection of his angels. I felt overjoyed, when I realized that the Holy Trinity also needs us, his children here on earth, just as a father and mother need their children.

We are his instruments

God doesn't have any other hands, any other hearts, any other ears. We are his helping, soothing, caressing and healing hands. We are his loving heart. We are the ear that attends a friend in distress with our full attention. We are his counterpart, his representative here on earth. We don't put the blame on any God for the "bad" that happens on earth. We are all working together at preserving the earth. However, God intervenes now and then in his truthfulness and sincerity, giving us a wake-up call, to put us back on track. Without these corrections to straighten us out, we would no longer be here. The three-in-one God, who is love in all, places the gifts in our hearts. We are the ones who must keep an open heart. And we make his earth a better place by enriching it with his gifts to us. All he asks of us is to follow his instructions intensifying love. This is his will and what he asks of us.

God = light = tone-sound-language of love.

If we follow our calling, our life-task, then we fill the earth with it, and keep the world in balance.

Taking a look at our earth and all life upon it, we become frightened, that far too many people, in a world that has become loud, don't hear their inner voice and overlook "the weeping eye of creation".

God speaks to us:

"Form a gigantic gold chain around the world (it should be made up of luminous souls and hearts)! Each human being and every animal makes up a link of the chain. Nobody – nothing – should be left out. Make a connecting bond occur around the whole world. Shake hands and unite in love! Stick together and free yourselves from all separation and condemnation! Only united as one are you strong!" And to this God added that regardless of all religions, all colours of skin and all languages, this should come about.

I have arrived at my home within me

On a long once dark and lonely path, which gradually turned out to be brighter and more loving, I was able to learn that the mastery of life is the result of acceptance and effort in all life's challenges and trials.

Thanks to my angels, in the most bitter hardship I found new ways of fulfillment in my life. Almost daily I used the methods I had learned to get over the hurdles along my way. The love, that I drew into my almost empty heart and darkened soul, had saved my life and put me back onto firm and stable legs of my own.

I believe and experience daily, that we find ourselves on track at mastering our lives when we recognize, that we can achieve happiness solely on a spiritual level and not in the body alone nor in materialism. Everything else, the material, deserves utmost respect. However, if we're seeking lasting happiness, it would be well to follow a higher ideal. If the decision has been made to take the spiritual path, there is no going back. This awareness of life-feeling of deep happiness is beyond comparison, and there is absolutely nothing else for which it could be exchanged.

One who has acquired love has everything he needs. He feels abundance within himself and experiences deep joy.

One day we will all return to the divine order and to the truth in our hearts

In the beginning was the God Spirit that is love.
And again in the end is the God Spirit, which
receives the spirit-soul into his love. From this love
we come, and to it we will return. Throughout the
course of our lives, we learn to entrust ourselves
into God's world by way of genuine words and
thoughts of love and to become one with God.

The mastery, in order to achieve it, doesn't tell us
how we can find it. No, we are asked flippantly:
"Who among you is going to do it?" And we are
told, it would be wise to take the protective sheath
of love with us along the way. Everyone must find
his own way.

In stillness, we experience, feel and hear

Each and every step will be made known to us. If
we live wholeheartedly, in honesty and have a pure
heart, we hear the fine and gentle harmonious tones
of the heavenly voices.

"Your life-task," the angels say, "is to earn your
own money with the talent that has been given to

you, and listen every moment what is asked of you."

The truth in my heart changed me and allowed me to master my life from then on till this very day.

And I ask God to continue bestowing me with grace, to live and be happy within the roots of my foundation and my inner heaven.

In the life of a person, on the emotional-spiritual level, there is nothing higher, nothing more sacred than to aquire heaven on earth, to dwell there full of enthusiasm until the end of this earthly existence, and to develop yet a still deeper love for oneself and for others.

The human being who has worked his way continuously through a thousand walls on his way to heaven, who has found his life-task, who fills his heart and the heart of the world with joy, who earns his living in this manner, this person has truly become the master of his life; he's "made" it.

It's up to us to open our hearts to a life full of love.

It's up to God to grant living beings the gift of love's mercy.

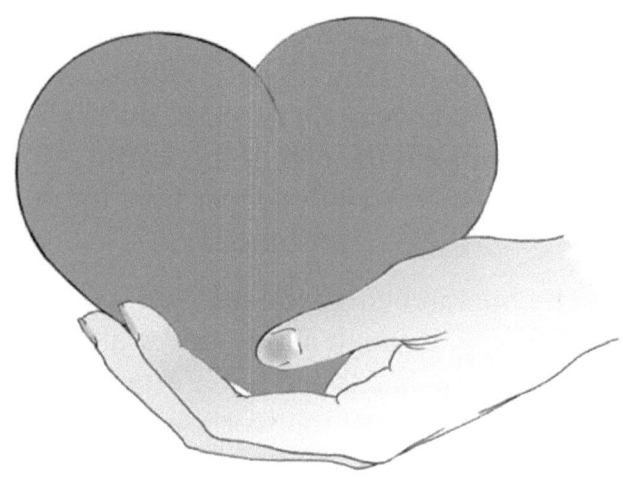

On the subject of healing the heart by the opening of it, I needed still more clarity.

I was aware of many almost dead and lost souls knowing I couldn't help them all.

During the night of January 17, 2012 God answered:

"People spend most of their time in life becoming immovable because of their hardened hearts. It's like hoarding gold and out of fear erecting more and more safety walls around the gold."

Open yourselves! Come out! Bring your treasures into the light!

The angels say: "More than 50 percent of the people on earth are afraid of their greatness, of what they are capable of doing. Instead they shut themselves in!"

The parable of Lazarus, a wealthy man, being raised from the dead, already touched me in my youth. I longed to understand the meaning of it.

Jesus, a friend of Lazarus, asked the rich business man to follow the path of love and give up all his possessions. (Certainly love does not call for a wealthy man to leave everything he owns behind. Love works in other ways. Love is humble, for in its fulfillment, it lacks nothing. Love feels rich. Love serves our talent and in return receives good payment. It doesn't exchange heart-healthiness for all the goods and money of the world. For love, inner peace is more important).

Lazarus didn't choose Jesus and his love. Jesus took leave and went on his way. Just a few days later the news of the death of his friend caught up with him. Jesus then returned to the house of Lazarus. When he arrived and was met by the grieving sisters, Mary and Martha, they scolded him: "If you had been here, our brother would not have died!" Jesus wished to be led to the tomb, where his friend was buried. He was deeply moved and called out in a loud voice: "Lazarus, come out!" Three times his call went out and through the thick walls of the tomb. The "dead" man came out and stepped into the light.
(Joh. 11)

I believe I'm able to interpret this parable today. Without a doubt it expresses how only the calling of the spirit of love can bring back to life the many worked-to-death, burned out, lifeless people, the almost dead and lost souls. This spirit of love brings them new vitality.

Love calls out to us: "Open up your walls from within! Come out into the light you nearly dead and lost souls! Quit working yourselves to death! Start living!"

"Give me your heart, and lay your life in my hands," God added.

From that hour on and to this day, I go out into the night and raise my hands toward the heavens to lay my heart, along with the hearts of my friends and sick and burdened ones into the healing spirit of God. Then I pray and say the words: "Bless all the hearts, bless every home. Thank you!"

"Thereby God will preserve the earth," the angels answered in March 2015.

It is a deep concern of mine, to persuade as many people as possible to stand at an open window at night before going to bed, and ask the God of love for a free and open heart. Let's all stick together, and lay this blessing in all of our hearts.

I sense that my words will be heard. And I know that God hears everyone when they talk to him from their heart.

It's amazing how liberation takes place within such a short time. God bids all human beings "to take their hearts in their hands" and deliver them to him for healing, in every need, over and over again.

"If you don't turn back and become like children, you'll never enter the Kingdom of Heaven."
(Jesus of Nazareth)

"I'll grant you the light of love if you give me your hearts, so that I may heal them."

It's never too late.

"Heaven mourns the all but dead and lost souls. So many people run past the essentials of life," the angels say. They ask us from deep within their hearts:

"Let us look all together to the "sun" and change the values in this new light!"

Heaven is here on earth, inside of us. It is our life-task to acquire this heaven, mentally and spiritually, to be able to lovingly enrich the earth with our talent. Taking this path is worth it; the earnings are remarkable. This is where a life of ease begins. To abide in heaven on earth means to accept the challenge with your right hand, and at the same time experience awareness with the left hand.

"Kind hearted human beings feel fine," heaven says. Those living in heaven on earth don't cling to anything. They trust in the flow of life, which says, that what is old and used up may go, to make room for the new.

Don't rest on your laurels

"Be a gift!"

"Be whole and become fulfilled and give yourself to the earth in return."

That is the plan.

I give my happiness to others and satisfy the hearts of those who are in need of fulfillment. According to God's plan, each one of us should be a gift to one another, taking part in each other's becoming whole through kind words, thoughts and deeds. We may do so as long as the weakened person needs us, until he is self-confident and can stand on his own feet.

Many people take off and follow their hearts in their very own original way. And this is a great thing for the world. This start into a new life is healing for the spirit-souls and their lives. A healthy spirit-soul spreads itself further and further and it can heal the whole world and dry the tears of heaven, if more and more people join in.

The hatred in the hearts of mankind has poisoned the earth in some ways. Love coming from hearts that are open can heal the earth again.

Talent and grace

The world could be a place full of gifted people, if people would work at developing their own talents instead of looking at others with envy. Talent is given to us by the fiery thoughts of the spirit of God, and put into practice with the help of a loving heart. (Being well grounded is important!) When we open ourselves up, we can find our talents. You can't find your talent by thinking about it. There is no sense in brooding about it; brooding hinders it. Some don't recognize it because it seems so natural to them, and because it flows without requiring any extreme effort. When it comes to our talents we are unique. A world filled with talented, exceptionally gifted people would be:

A world following God's plan.

Heaven says: "At the moment, God is turning the world upside down. Everything is being renewed with people who are finding their way back to love, to build up a new earth in new harmony."

Everybody has an equal chance, by his own doing, to open up to his talent

Breathe! Breathe! Breathe!

Train yourself to having a volume of breath of seven litres.

If you fail having success doing this on your own then look for a person specialising among other things in breathing techniques. Yoga teachers are also well-trained in breathing exercises. Either outdoors or at an open window, close one nostril with the thumb, and breathe in strongly through the other nostril. Breathe out through the open mouth. Then close the other nostril, again breathe in strongly through the open nostril and then out through the open mouth. Your head becomes free, your intellectual powers sharpened and your spirit fired up for action.

Listen to music! Make music!

Move your body! Dance! Sing! Laugh! Shout! Be silent. Express your feelings, the truth that's in your heart!

Connect with the strength that brings out the good in you!

Get started. Give your soul enough inner space, comparable to a spacious castle, so that it can unfold to it's utmost.

Wrap a protective sheath of love around yourself, the Selflove you have acquired! You will need it in case someone tries to offend you. Be prepared for those envious people who will try to attack your castle. Be aware and wise! Be ready and watch out well for yourself! Stay in your inner castle, in your centre! Remain in your light of love! Open all the doors and windows! Be open! No more "walls"! You are no longer that helpless child whose light, the brightly lit soul and pure spirit, can be destroyed.

You have serenity. Your soul is well anchored. You have learned who you are, and that you are under the angels' protection, when you believe. You don't let your security be shaken. You have learned to accept all challenges, to grow with them, and have become clever and wise along your journey leading you to Selflove. You have come to realize that the offender is not following his life's plan. Filled with anger and grief for himself and his unfulfilled life, he blames God and the world. Instead of taking responsibility for his own life, he assaults others. Realize that the offender is imbalanced. He's still out on the rough path that you were once travelling.

Don't quarrel, don't fight, don't judge!

Understand that it's fear and not love that tackles you!

Be alert! In dangerous situations, be the guardian of your heart, your mind and your soul! When a "fight" presents itself refrain from bitterness and anger. Your heart would suffer from the damage. Once again it would have to build up a wall.

Intensify your inner light!

You've learned how to operate the light switch:

The bright mind of "I love, respect and acknowledge myself with all my heart," that you say to yourself

10 times - 100 times - 1000 times

strengthens your light, multiplies your strength and with this power you are able to let go and proceed peacefully along your way. Never be arrogant in your thoughts! Your feet leave the ground in arrogance, causing you eventually to fall. Haughtiness precedes a fall.

Trust that the offender as well will find the path to happiness!

Direct your focus on the goodness in him, take "his heart in your hands," place it in God's hands for a curative blessing, and help him to see the good in himself, if you're able to. In this way, you build a heaven for yourself and your heart and contribute to the sustainability of the earth for yourself, your dear ones and your children.

"Perceive him and he will feel the truth in himself!"

It's OK to get ahead of your primary family

Many a time it occurs that several members of a family preoccupy themselves with the problems and catastrophes of the world and get stuck in their harm, putting all their energy into that harm. Whereas other family members go along their way living their gifts and talents happily and full of enthusiasm. They draw their power out of their own hearts. Have the courage to pass by the stagnant pessimists who tell you what a bad place the world is. Allow yourself to say to them that they should start by cleaning up their own act. If they will listen to you, point out to them that their destructive thinking is making them ill and evokes a mood of doom and gloom.

Tackle what needs to be taken care of in your life. Let go. Don't hang on to the past and things you no longer need. The past holds no energy and is motionless. The past is without air and therefore fixed. Look ahead and be free. Only when you're free can you be active in an ingenious and creatively unique manner. And if you're free, you give the freedom to all others.

You are the most important person in your life. Simply quit waiting and hoping for something to happen. Get busy, be yourself, and be a role model for others. Infect others with your ability for enthusiasm and your faith in goodness. Be their support and happiness for a while.

Every creature is very special and brilliant in the "eyes of love". Be brave and open yourself up to what is very special and grand.

Be a golden link in the golden chain!

If YOU are missing, the chain is incomplete.

Abide

with Mother Earth,

with the light of a loving heart,

with the power of a healthy mind,

in contact with the influx of magical powers.

Thereby, you live with all other creatures united in love.

If you love your life, you receive the strength to live from this love.

"I love my life and my life loves me!"

Selflove is your protection, your security in your life!

You will master your life, when love is within you and all around you!

Peace is alive within you, when you do what your inner truth demands of you.

Think, but don't think too much.
After all, it turns out the way
God, in his love for you, wants it to.

THANKS BE TO GOD!

SDG

About my life-task:

God spoke to me saying: "I need you as a helping soul for all my nearly dead and lost souls here on earth. You must show them the way to love themselves and all others, to live a happy and a good life in freedom and understanding. Help these people to come alive and find their way. Fill their hearts with love ..." I had no idea of my life's task.

At the time, I took note of the message, although I didn't understand it.

This was soon to change. The angels led me to a self-help-program. First and foremost, I had to see to it that I rid myself of my struggles and compulsions. I didn't yet know that I had to lead the way – from darkness into the light – in order to qualify for my life-task, and to become strong.

The powers of heaven and earth have been carrying me through a hell on earth in order to be of service to them as soon as possible.

God moves in mysterious ways!

Finding myself at rock bottom and faced with rough turns along the way, my belief in a divine plan nearly abandoned me.

Today, I know that I had to be trained and tested to be able to encourage others to keep going along the toughest paths in their lives and to keep an eye on their goal.

Heaven hears and sees you when you are out and about with goodness in mind.

About me

At age 13, I first became consciously aware of my body.

It was incredible what I discovered.

I stood in front of the mirror and couldn't believe what I saw.

I saw a slender, tall, attractive young woman with beautiful long legs.

Her delicate body, her long hair almost reaching her waist, pretty face with fine skin, gave her an attractive appearance.

For just a moment, I was able to feel deep happiness.

I had been recovering from the hellish experiences of my childhood allowing me to feel this happiness when a thick, constricting net fell upon me, choking me. Why couldn't I get up? Why shouldn't I be allowed to take part in a happy life?

How often I had to hear „Go away, we can't stand you, and a lot more harmful words that can bring a human being down mentally-spiritually, until he finally collapses and snaps.

At the time, I wasn't able to interpret it as a huge amount of jealousy.

Today, we would call it mobbing, terrorising, tyranny.

I believed that I was unbearable and unacceptable.

I ran away from myself and my burning pain. And soon I saw myself through the eyes of others.

I began to destroy myself by letting my eating habits slip into what was abnormal. I stuffed myself with chocolate and all kinds of cheap candy and any kind of junk food and gained 20 kg in less than a few months. Hatred, self-denial and self-contempt accompanied me day and night. I was trapped in some "sort of strange mind".

I was no longer myself and I didn't realize that I was ill.

Over a period of more than 20 years, I slipped from excessive eating habits into phases of depression, sometimes even without eating.

Control mechanisms, thoughts of suicide and other illnesses of the mind, that affect the body, took control of my young life.

I had reached the critical stage of spiritual and mental emptiness.

The infirmity of anorexia, the addiction which seeks fulfillment and freedom, had taken hold of me.

After 23 years of hell, I came across a book on the subject of loving yourself: Louise Hay "You Can Heal Your Life."

Louise Hay wrote about loving yourself and I worked out a way to get there.

Every evening, I placed a candle next to me in front of the mirror in my bathroom. I looked into my eyes and said to myself: "I love, respect and acknowledge you with all my heart, and I swear that one day you'll be a healthy kind of slender and a healthy Waltraud once again". And this new Waltraud will be better and stronger than ever before!"

At the same time, I crossed my hands over my heart giving this order to that special place deep inside me: "Did you understand me?! That's the way we're going to do it!"

I put all the strength I had into my words and only quit when tears were running down my face.

For me, my eyes were like walls, and I sensed that underneath the tough layers that had to be worked through, something very valuable, fine, beautiful and loving was living there. I felt a deep longing for myself.

It took full concentration and all my ambition to free this sensitive and frightened being.

After weeks of work in front of the mirror, the walls within me began to crumble piece by piece, and I started to notice something happening in my throat and chest area.

My soul gained its life back.

My healthy consciousness received light and defended itself within me. I felt all the anger, and sadness behind it, that I had swallowed and suppressed years ago. I needed to set up new rules in my head.

I gave myself the order, "This eternal and unchanging, tiring chatter, pulling me down, has to stop."

I traded the old spirit for a new one. But it took time. According to the signs of the zodiac, those born in Taurus, the bull, can pursue and accomplish something in a consistently stubborn and straight-forward manner, once they have made the decision.

Step by step, I shovelled my way free with untiring commitment. From then on, new and constructive thoughts filled my heart and my soul with life, a life of love.

Even today, in an "emergency", I work with the mirror and lay my hands on my heart and stomach. I let the love coming from my spirit flow into them, and I don't stop until my tears have cleansed the channels.

Every crying spell is a releasing of something from the past, an opening of closed off channels, taking one to a deeper level.

And so I reach a depth in my heart I had never imagined. Here is where I take the strength that I need to live.

My life today is fulfilled with love and so beautiful. I am filled with happiness and gratitude due to having walked the path and finding myself again.

Personal development takes place up until our very last breath has been drawn. By facing all the challenges, each step becomes easier and freer.

When refusing developmental processes, I suffer a relapse and must painfully start all over again from the beginning with the same experiences until I've understood the lesson.

For many years, a sick mind with all its trickery had a hold on me.

A negative power was controlling me.

I took my life into my own hands. Today, I am in charge of my thoughts and actions.

If just for a moment, I believe I can hold on tightly to life and wish to control it, or have to control it, nail it down securely, it is precisely at this moment when it slips away from me. I can enjoy life and let it flow. Filled with humility and devotion, I recognize the power of a higher love that accompanies my healthy life today along with my heart and soul, making my life fulfilling, guiding me right into the middle of happiness, day after day, after day!

I've become a happy person in this awareness:

I can't please everyone. I can "only" be true to my own heart, and I no longer make other people's problems my problems.

My life is bubbling over with gratitude.

Space for personal notes of your mastery, your path to a happy and fulfilled life

How to breathe seven litres:

lie down on the floor,

stretch your arms and your legs in opposite directions,

as much as possible,

while breathing in.

Relax while breathing out.

After 10 rounds feel into the body and realize the light and the grounding from head to toe.